THE FACTS ABOUT

SINGLE-PARENT FAMILIES

BY
Marilyn Bailey

EDITED BY
Anita Larsen

CONSULTANT
Elaine Wynne, M.A., Licensed Psychologist

New York

CIP
LIBRARY OF CONGRESS CATALOGING IN PUBLICATION DATA

Bailey, Marilyn
  Single-parent families.

  (The facts about)
  Includes index.
  SUMMARY: Discusses the myths and misconceptions that sometimes surround single-parent families.
  1. Children of single parents — United States — Juvenile literature. 2. Children of divorced parents — United States — Juvenile literature. 3. Single-parent family — United States — Juvenile literature. [1. Single-parent family. 2. Family life.] I. Larsen, Anita. II. Title. III. Series.
  HQ777.4.B35   1989   306.85'6—dc20   89-1415
  ISBN 0-89686-437-5

PHOTO CREDITS

Cover: Third Coast Stock Source: Kent DuFault
Third Coast Stock Source: (Kent DuFault) 4, 30; (Thomas Edwards) 6; (William Meyer) 21; (Jeff Lowe) 24; (MacDonald Photography) 37, 40
DRK Photo: (Don & Pat Valenti) 11; (Randy Trine) 19
The Image Works: (Bob Daemmrich) 15, 33, 44; (Mark Antman) 29
Berg & Associates: (Kirk Schlea) 16

Copyright © 1989 by Crestwood House, Macmillan Publishing Company

All rights reserved. No part of this book may be reproduced or transmitted in any form or by any means, electronic or mechanical, including photocopying, recording, or by any information storage and retrieval system, without permission in writing from the Publisher.

Macmillan Publishing Company
866 Third Avenue
New York, NY 10022
Collier Macmillan Canada, Inc.

Produced by Carnival Enterprises
Printed in the United States of America
First Edition
10 9 8 7 6 5 4 3 2 1

TABLE OF CONTENTS

Jeff 5
A New Kind of Family............................ 7
What Is a Family? 10
Why Is the Family Changing Now? 14
Living with Mom 15
Living with Dad 17
Living Here, Visiting There 20
One Family, Two Homes 23
Living with Somebody Else....................... 24
Tough Beginnings............................... 25
Things Get Better 28
A New Idea of What Family Means................ 31
Stories and Misconceptions 32
Some Problems Single-Parent Families Have........ 36
Some Solutions................................. 38
Scary Problems and Who Can Help 41
The Bright Side................................. 43
For More Information 46
Glossary/Index................................47-48

JEFF

It was the night of the school play. Jeff inched the stage curtain aside and looked for his mother among the crowd filling the old gym. Behind him, costumes rustled. A shoe squeaked against the stage floor. The pasty smell of greasepaint mixed with the dust of the faded red curtain.

Men and women, walking together, entered the gym. Some had small children with them. After one couple sat down, a little boy climbed onto the man's lap.

Jeff felt the familiar ache just below his ribs. He wondered what it felt like to have your father hold you.

He would never know. His father had left before he was born, before his mother even knew she was pregnant.

Jeff blinked. His eyes hurt from staring at the gym door. It was silly, he knew, to think his mother would come if he just stared hard enough. She had two jobs. She had warned Jeff she might not be able to get time off. They were busy at work.

Jeff wished she could quit her night job. He mowed lawns, raked leaves, and shoveled snow in order to buy his own clothes. Still they could afford only a one-bedroom apartment. But this one was larger than the last. Jeff's bed was the sofa in the living room, but he had some privacy. Two bookcases screened it from the rest of the room. The new school was better, too. Other kids in Jeff's class lived with only one parent.

Single-parent families are neither bad nor good. They are simply different.

Today, four out of ten children live with one parent.

He watched as more people came into the gym, moms and dads together. Then Jeff saw his mother. He sighed. She had made it. She walked to the third row where Jill's father sat with the mothers of six more of Jeff's classmates. This group always sat together at school events. They were different from the other parents of Jeff's classmates. They were single parents.

In Jeff's class of 30, 8 kids lived in *single-parent families*. The other 22 kids lived with both parents.

Today, four out of ten kids will live with only one parent some time in their lives, according to *social sci-*

entists. Social scientists study how people live and the way their lives change and why.

Children in single-parent families are often called *single-parent kids*, or *s-p kids*, for short. *One-parent kids* is another term used. In 1960, when Jeff's mother was born, about four kids out of thirty were s-p kids. In 1970, six out of thirty kids lived with one parent. By the year 2000, social scientists predict that half of all children will live in single-parent families some time in their lives.

Why are families changing? What is life like in a single-parent family? Which parent does a child live with? How is living with a mom different from living with a dad? What happens if a child can't live with either parent?

A NEW KIND OF FAMILY

Single-parent families are a new family form. The term single-parent family isn't really correct for many of these families, according to social scientists. Most s-p kids are children of divorced parents. They have two parents. But their parents live in separate *households*. A more accurate term is *single-parent household*.

But the term single-parent family has come to mean a family in which children live with one parent at a time, like Nick and his younger sister, Missy.

They lived with their parents in California. One day, their mother explained that she and their father were going to separate. "I'm going to move to Connecticut," she said. "You can come with me or stay with your dad."

Nick and Missy chose to go with their mother. Soon, they were living in a single-parent family.

Like Nick and Missy, most s-p kids (90 percent) live with their mothers. Six out of ten s-p kids are children of divorced or separated parents.

About two out of ten children, like Jeff, live with mothers who have never married. These mothers may have decided not to marry and still have children. Or they may have become pregnant and then decided not to marry. The number of unmarried mothers is growing. There are ten times as many now as there were in 1960.

Some children live in single-parent families because one parent has died. Others are s-p kids because a parent is in jail or a mental hospital.

An s-p kid may also live with someone other than a parent. Kevin lives with his grandmother. His mother was very young when he was born. Kevin's grandmother took care of him while his mother finished school. Even after Kevin's mother got a job and moved into her own apartment, Kevin continued to live with his grandmother. Kevin likes it. His grandmother seems like his mother. His mother seems like a sister who visits him every weekend.

A few s-p kids live with people not related to them.

In the case of divorce, social scientists call the parent with whom a child lives the *live-in parent*. The one with whom the child doesn't live is referred to as the *absent parent*, even though that parent may still visit.

When parents divorce, the court rules which parent children will live with. The judge awards *custody* to one parent and gives *visitation rights* to the other.

Custody means guardianship and care. The parent with custody is responsible for taking care of the children and makes all the decisions concerning them. Sometimes, as in Nick and Missy's case, parents and the court allow children to decide with which parent they will live.

Usually, however, the court decides. In most cases, it gives mothers custody. Only a few s-p kids live with their fathers. But the number is growing. In 1960, only about 3 out of 100 children lived with their fathers. Today, about 10 out of 100 do.

Visitation rights mean that the parent who does not have custody of the children has the right to visit them. The court may say when and how long the visits can be, or parents may work that out themselves.

As often as possible, courts award parents *joint custody*. Then both parents are responsible for the children, just as they were when the family lived in one house. Children spend almost equal time with both parents.

The court also decides where the money to raise children will come from. This money is called *child support*.

In most cases, parents share the cost of raising the children. Generally, however, fathers pay more because they earn more. This will change as more women begin to earn better salaries. Today, most children live with mothers, and fathers pay child support.

Single-parent families are neither bad nor good. They are only different. Like other families, they feel love and face problems, have fun and do chores, go through good times and bad, fight and enjoy each other. Everything may not be the same as when parents lived together, but somehow it can work. Single-parent families are still families.

WHAT IS A FAMILY?

A family is a group of people related by blood, marriage, or adoption. For thousands of years "family" to most people meant a married man and woman and their children.

But it wasn't always that way.

Back in the dark corners of time, when all we know about history comes from pictures people drew on cave walls, there were families. But no one called them families. People did what they did to stay alive.

Basically, people had two instincts: the instinct to sur-

For many years, a family meant a married woman and man and their children. Today that definition is changing.

vive and the instinct to reproduce, to have children in order to keep the human race alive. Nobody talked about love. People used all their energy to survive harsh weather, to find food and a place to live, and to keep children alive.

Then men figured out how they were related to children. They started staying with the mother of their children to prove *paternity*, to prove which children were theirs. Women allowed this because it made raising the children easier. Thus, families came into being.

As men and women stayed together to raise their children, affection for each other grew. People learned to become *intimate*. At the same time, proving which children belonged to which man became very important. In those days, when a man married, his wife and children were his property. He owned them. He could put his children to work in his fields or give his children into slavery or marriage. So, men and women took vows in public in a ceremony now called marriage.

As time passed, families began to arrange marriages to gain property or protect it. A son from one wealthy family married a daughter of another wealthy family. When parents died, the new family owned the property of both the old families.

Having property has meant having power in most countries. People have used marriage in many different ways to get or keep it. Early in Egypt's history, brothers married sisters to keep property in the family. In Tibet, even today, when her husband dies, a woman marries his brother for the same reason.

In India, China, and Africa, men were allowed to marry several wives. That way they could have several families, more children, and more property. In some areas of India and Africa, such families still exist.

At different times in history, men have also had several wives at once because there were many more women in a community than men. This happened when disasters, such as war, floods, or earthquakes, killed many of the people in a community. They wanted more children in order to increase the population again.

Men have also had more than one wife for religious reasons. The Mormon religion, for instance, encouraged such marriages. In the United States in the 1800s, Mormon men (mainly in Utah) had more than one wife. They believed if a man had many children, his reward in his life after death was greater. The majority of Americans didn't like this idea, so the federal government passed a law against it. Every few years, however, newspapers report the discovery of communities that still encourage such marriages today.

Throughout history, men have wanted families and children for several other reasons as well: to make themselves strong politically, to honor their ancestors, to look after their property and work their land, and to pray for them when they were dead. At different times, men who had many children were also thought to be "better" men than those who didn't.

But men didn't always marry the women by whom

they had children. In China, for many years, wealthy families included *concubines*. These women were not wives. Their role was to provide children. Sometimes, such families had a hundred members. But always important in those large households was what the Chinese called the "little family"—mother, father, and children.

In the United States, the "little family" always has been important. But people's needs are changing, so the form of the family is changing, too.

WHY IS THE FAMILY CHANGING NOW?

The family is changing in this country chiefly because of divorce. The first divorce recorded in the United States was in the early 1600s, soon after Plymouth Colony was settled. By 1804, one marriage in 100 ended in divorce. By the end of the 1920s, it was one in six. Today, one in two or three marriages breaks up.

Divorces are increasing because the way people live is changing. Once the family provided everything its members needed. The family grew its own food, made its own clothing, and educated its young, and the father ruled and protected the family. Today, however, most families buy what they need. Fathers and many mothers, too, work outside the home.

Women have discovered they can take care of themselves—and their children—if they choose. And society also says it's "okay" for single women—and men—to have children. So marriage isn't necessary to the family for the reasons it once was. Families still exist, but they are changing form. One new form is the single-parent family. Single-parent families themselves come in different sizes and shapes.

LIVING WITH MOM

Living with Mom presents problems that range from silly to serious. Children who no longer live with their

Divorce is becoming more common and is one reason why there are many single-parent families.

Some single-parent kids fear their mothers won't be able to take care of things. Others fear their moms will leave them.

fathers worry about many things at first: Who's going to carve the meat, put on the storm windows, get the car fixed? Who's going to protect them from prowlers? What if they don't have enough money to buy food?

Not having enough money is, in fact, the biggest and most common problem children face when their parents separate. Almost every family's life-style changes. For some, that means no more designer jeans or new albums. For others, it's worse.

Debbie and Cal's father didn't pay child support. Their mother had to work two jobs. They also had to move into an unsafe neighborhood. Debbie was so afraid of prowlers she slept with a baseball bat beside her bed.

When a friend put strong locks on all the windows and the door, Debbie was still afraid. Then she realized what she was really frightened of. She was afraid her mother couldn't handle things. She was afraid her mother wouldn't be able to take care of her and her brother. She was afraid her mother would run away as Debbie's father had.

Many s-p kids are afraid the remaining parent will die or leave them. Like Debbie, most get over that fear. They see that their mothers can handle things. They learn where to get help when they need it.

Some fathers run away when the family breaks up. They think they've failed their families, that their children will be better off without them. After a time, though, many fathers miss their children. They get in touch with them and keep in touch.

LIVING WITH DAD

Only one in ten s-p kids lives with his or her father. Courts usually award custody to mothers. Many judges still think only mothers know how to take care of children. In fact, in most families, the mother *is* the nurturer. She listens to her children and helps them take care of problems, even when she works outside the home. Another reason fathers haven't been given custody in the past is because mothers were made to feel guilty if they "gave up" their children to fathers. This picture is beginning to change. Many women have careers and are willing to give fathers custody of children. In addition, many men are learning to be nurturers. More of them are asking courts for custody of their children.

Being able to talk to their fathers is one of the things kids living with Dad worry about. Most haven't done it before, but need. brings about change. Even if their mothers visit regularly, they aren't around all the time. So the children learn how to talk to their fathers, and their fathers learn how to listen. And life is better. Much better.

"I found out Dad isn't some super-somebody who knows how to do everything like I thought he was," 12-year-old Tony says. "He had to figure out how to do a lot of stuff around the house after Mom moved out. And he goofed a lot. Now he doesn't get so mad when I mess something up." Dads and kids get to know each other as they might not have in two-parent families.

Kids also worry about their fathers not being able to cook. As with talking, though, both fathers and their children soon learn how to do it.

Steve has another problem. "I hate being a maid," he says. "I have to do the grocery shopping and clean the house. I have to take care of my little brother and sisters until Dad comes home."

Single-parent kids who live with their fathers occasionally worry that they will not be able to talk to their fathers as easily as they could talk to their mothers.

Most s-p kids do more chores than kids in two-parent families. At first, they grumble about that. Later, they're glad. They feel better prepared for life than many two-parent kids.

Children who live with their dads often miss their mothers, of course. But they usually learn to deal with that as well. Betsy has lived with her dad since her mother died. "I think about her a lot," she explains. "Especially at night. I keep wondering what it would be like if she hadn't died. Sometimes I feel really close to her. Whenever I get in a tough spot, I ask myself what Mom would do."

"When you lose a parent, it really hurts," Carrie, age thirteen, says. Her mother ran away when Carrie was three. "Sometimes I wonder what she's doing, where she's living, what her life's like. I wonder if she thinks about me. I used to feel really rejected. I don't anymore because I have Dad. He loves me. We're really close. I still miss Mom. You never really get over the pain, but it gets smaller. It's like a big freckle on your hand. It's always there, but sometimes you don't notice it."

LIVING HERE, VISITING THERE

How often children see their absent parents varies. Ellen, Joe, and Lindy live with their mothers. Joe visits his father every weekend. Ellen visits her father every other weekend. Lindy sees her father once a month when he comes into town. Carla lives with her dad and visits her mother every Sunday.

Visiting can be tricky. Sometimes parents fight during the divorce, and their children get caught in the middle. Then visiting can be miserable.

"My mom and dad always ask what the other one is doing," Carla admits. "They want to know if the other one has bought something new."

"You have to quit answering their questions," Joe explains. "Anyway, it gets better after a while."

S-p kids can still have other problems, however.

Joe rides the bus two hours to see his dad. He gets tired of going back and forth all the time. Sometimes he wants to skip the visits.

Lindy's father lives in the country. She can't find anything to do there.

"It makes you mad," Ellen says, "if you only see your dad every other weekend, and then he has a date and goes out one night. You'd think he could date enough when I'm not there."

Jack also lives with his dad. He says he doesn't mind

Many single-parent kids live with one parent but visit the other parent on weekends or during the summer.

giving up his weekend to be with his mother, but he hates feeling left out on Monday morning. His friends always talk about what they did together Saturday and Sunday.

Gretchen visits her dad only in the summer and during school vacations. "It was hard at first," she says. "I had to make new friends. I missed Mom. When I went home, I missed Dad. After a couple of years, though, it got better. My friends at Dad's remember me now, and we do a lot of neat things together. I still miss whichever parent I'm not with, but we talk on the phone every week now so it's not as bad."

For kids like Gretchen, spending a long time with each parent is like having two homes. Usually, they have their own rooms at both houses. On the other hand, kids who make short visits may sleep on the sofa. They miss having their own space.

Most problems can be worked out if children and parents talk about them. Visiting times can be rearranged. Interesting activities can be planned. Parents can provide a little space or a trunk or chest of drawers for each child's special use.

One problem never goes away, however. S-p kids always think the other parent should be living with them. They learn, though, to concentrate on the good things in their lives and accept the problems that can't be solved. "Everybody has some problems," as Keith puts it.

Whatever problems visitation causes, most s-p kids are happy to be able to see the parent they don't live with.

ONE FAMILY, TWO HOMES

The best arrangement for many children of divorce is joint custody. Because each parent lives in a different house, they are still single-parent kids, but they see each parent often, usually in equal amounts of time. Their problems tend to be more manageable than those of children living primarily with one parent.

The solution to Cathy's problem, for instance, was simple. She likes to draw. But she always found her sketchbook at one house, her pencils at the other. So, her parents bought her two sets.

Todd, on the other hand, felt that one place had to be home. "I have to have a base," he says. "So I live with my mom, but I go over to my dad's almost every day."

The amount of time children spend at each house may vary. Mark's parents live close together. He spends a week with one, then a week with the other. He goes to the same school. He has different friends, though, in each neighborhood. He has more friends at his dad's, but he still wants to spend time with his mom.

Vivian's mother lives in Connecticut, her father in Arizona. She's been living with her mother for two years, spending summers and every other Christmas with her father. In two years, when she starts high school, she will live with her father and visit her mother summers and every other Christmas.

LIVING WITH SOMEBODY ELSE

Three out of ten single-parent kids live with someone other than a parent. Some, like Kevin, mentioned at the beginning of this book, live with grandmothers. Most don't know who their fathers are.

Some single-parent kids live with their grandparents instead of their mothers or fathers.

"Sometimes I look at a man on the street and wonder if he's my dad," Jamie says. "There's a spot inside me that's empty. It's where my dad belongs."

Norman knows who his father is, but he hasn't seen him since he was a baby. Norman lived with his mother, but they couldn't get along. Then he became friends with a teacher who wanted to adopt him. Norman's mother agreed. She visits Norman often, and they get along better than they did when they lived together.

TOUGH BEGINNINGS

The histories of single-parent families are as different from each other as those of two-parent families. A few become single-parent families through choice, for instance. Unmarried men adopt children. Women choose to have children without getting married. These families have time to prepare for their lives. Most single-parent families do not.

Most single-parent families have abrupt beginnings. They come about through divorce, death, or *desertion*. A few happen when one parent goes to jail or a mental institution. For these single-parent families, the first days are tough.

Everyone has new roles to fill, but nobody knows at first what his or her role is. A mother is no longer just a mother, or a father a father. For a time, he or she must be both parents. One parent must do everything the absent parent used to do. Because parents often feel off balance emotionally, they may act in unfamiliar ways.

A parent who doesn't live with his or her child may become distant and seem just like another grown-up. A live-in parent might begin to drink too much or go out often. Another might go on a health or cleanliness kick, change jobs, change hairstyles, or go back to school. And, of course, either parent might date or spend time with different people. Even if they do none of these things, at least for a while they aren't the parents their children once knew.

Sally's mother was sick for two years before she died. "I knew she was going to die," Sally says. "Dad and I had been doing all the housework and cooking. When she died, Dad kept saying it was a blessing because she'd been so sick. But then he would cry. He'd get the vacuum out, then stand there and look at it as if he didn't know how it worked. It was scary. Dad always knew how to do everything."

When parents change like this, children often feel as if nothing will ever be right again. But life goes on. Everybody has to eat, sleep, have clean clothes, go to school, do homework, and go to work. Children often learn to take better care of themselves.

Yet inside, feelings are tearing them apart:

- "How could they have done this to me?"
- "I was afraid of what was going to happen."

- "I was afraid I might never see my dad again."
- "I felt guilty. Maybe it was my fault that my parents couldn't get along."

Most are sad, grieving not only for what is lost but for what will never be.

"It was havoc," Kelly remembers. "We had pizza for dinner for two months. My mom didn't want to cook, and we kids didn't want to sit around a table. There'd be that empty spot there where Dad should have been. We were going to visit Yellowstone next summer. Now we can't go."

Children also can feel mixed emotions when the family changes.

"It was hard," Wally says. "We had to move. I had to change schools twice in six months. But it was a relief, too. My parents yelled and screamed at each other all the time. They were mean to each other. When they weren't fighting, it was like waiting for the roof to fall in. So it was a relief."

Relief is often common when the absent parent is an alcoholic. But relief can be riddled with guilt. Kids think they aren't "supposed to" feel glad that one parent is gone, even though it is natural. And when an abusive parent dies, children feel both relief and guilt, even while they feel sad.

Schoolwork often suffers. Kids are more apt to get into trouble in school. They need time to find out what belonging to this new family means. They need to find out who they really are.

The adjustment is less painful if parents have explained what's going on. That doesn't happen often. Both before and after divorce or death, the parent is having a hard time, too.

Counselors or family therapists can help kids make sense of these common problems and feelings. Their advice can help make the adjustment period easier:

- "Remember that your parents are human, too. If you feel down, go and give your parent a hug. You'll both feel better."
- "Talk about your feelings. Ask questions about what has happened."
- "Brooding too long about your single-parent status is a waste of emotional resources. Try to feel good about yourself."
- "If your parent's problems become more than you can handle, get some help."

THINGS GET BETTER

In six months, life becomes a little easier. Everyone calms down, chores get done, meals get back to normal, emergencies are handled, and problems get solved. Parents aren't so angry with each other. They're ready to talk to their children about what has happened. Visi-

It usually takes a few months for people to adjust to a death or a divorce. But eventually, everyone adjusts and parents and their children can talk about the changes.

tation schedules are arranged. Children find it easier to talk to their friends about what's going on.

"It's as if you step over the past and try to forget the worst that happened," Gail says. "But you're always aware that someone is missing."

Occasionally, kids get caught between parents who are still bickering. One parent asks questions about the other. Or a parent still feels guilty and tries to "buy" the child's love or loyalty.

Even when parents are friendly, visitation can be dif-

29

ficult. The absent parent is in new surroundings, associating with new people. Kids have to work harder to have a good relationship, but they find it worth the effort.

"You really grow up during those six months," Jill says. "You still wish the other parent was there, but you can see kids are doing something with their dad without crying. Sometimes, though, you still cry later at home."

Angie has learned not to dwell on problems. "I take it as it is," she explains. "I know now that I'm not the only kid who has gone through this, so I don't feel so alone anymore."

A NEW IDEA OF WHAT FAMILY MEANS

As time goes on, s-p kids get a new idea of what family means. They learn they can get the love and attention they need in a single-parent family. In fact, life is sometimes easier with only one parent making the decisions.

"It's not 'Go ask your father' or 'See what your mother thinks,' " according to Paula, 11.

S-p kids learn they still have two parents. Divorce doesn't erase one parent, leaving the other alone. Parents just live in different houses or apartments.

Even when a parent dies or leaves and never comes

Some kids think living with just one parent is easier than living with both parents.

back, the influence of that parent is still there. Relatives may still say, "You look just like your father." Or a father may say, "You're just like your mother. She was always good at mathematics."

For some children, life is better in a single-parent family. When parents fight or find it difficult to stay married, a two-parent family lives in stress and tension. There may be less care for kids, or even no care, in such cases. When the tension is removed, both parents are usually able to give their children the love and attention they need. Sometimes the tension can be removed only by divorce.

Children develop new relationships with their parents in single-parent family situations. S-p children can become closer to the live-in parent than they were when in the two-parent family. They do more things together. When good relations are continued with the absent parent, they may even spend more time and do more things with that parent, too.

STORIES AND MISCONCEPTIONS

Does broken home *mean broken child? Do children from broken homes do badly in school or get into trouble?*

No, say the experts.

Single-parent kids often become closer to the parent they live with than to the parent they only visit.

"The term 'broken home' is misleading," says one social scientist. "It implies that the family is broken. Divorce breaks up a household, not a family." Mom is still Mom. Dad is still Dad.

A study done in 1979 by an Association of School Principals did find that children of broken homes had a harder time at school. Their grades dropped, and they were more apt to be suspended.

"When you hear this," Eleanor says, "it makes you feel abnormal. If someone thinks you're abnormal, you can start to feel abnormal. We have feelings, too. We get angry, are sad, feel love. We have problems like peer pressure, alcohol, drugs, and sex, as well as emotional problems at home and school, just like kids in two-parent families do."

But, experts say, children growing up in unhappy two-parent homes suffer more than children in stable one-parent homes. In fact, they are apt to do worse in school than kids from broken homes.

In 1980, a parents' group conducted its own survey. It pointed out to educators the reasons for some trouble at school: S-p kids move around a lot, which means changing schools. S-p kids may have more problems at home. They said children from broken homes did badly in school because schools were often insensitive to their needs.

"It's a two-parent world," one single parent says. "But it's changing. Slowly."

Since then, schools have become more aware of the

needs of children from single-parent families. One principal, for instance, acknowledged that s-p kids do have trouble the first six months while they're adjusting to their new life-styles. After that, most kids get back into the swing.

Do boys raised by their mothers become sissies?

The problem with this question is in the definition of sissy. If boys don't go around acting tough, some people say they're sissies. But are they?

Society's idea that men "should" be tough or never need help is slowly changing. Men are becoming more sensitive to the needs of others. They are learning to develop the nurturing qualities of parenting. Boys raised by single mothers learn these qualities early.

But having *role models* is important, too, especially for teenagers. According to some social scientists, children living with same-sex parents are better adjusted than children living with opposite-sex parents. Boys living with fathers and girls with mothers feel better about themselves. They're more mature. They get along better with friends and can talk to people more easily. They're more cooperative.

Role models don't have to be fathers, however. They can be uncles, grandfathers, adult cousins or adult friends.

Are all single mothers on welfare?

No. Sixty-two percent of the mothers in single-parent families work. Others live on money received from insurance when their spouses died. When fathers do not support their children, however, some women have to go on welfare until they become adjusted or get more schooling to earn enough money to support their children.

And some mothers do remain on welfare. They may not be able to get jobs that pay enough to take care of their children. Or they may not know how to go about getting jobs. Others can't find or can't afford to pay someone to take care of their children while they work. They need help that society is slow to provide.

SOME PROBLEMS SINGLE-PARENT FAMILIES HAVE

Lack of money is the biggest problem for single-parent families headed by women. A Stanford University study shows what happens after divorce.

During the first year after divorce, women and children have 73 percent less money than they did during the marriage. If they had $200 a week to live on before divorce, they have less than $50 a week during the first year after the divorce.

Men, however, live better by almost 42 percent. If they had $200 before divorce, they have almost $300 after divorce.

In addition, more than one-half of the women awarded child support by the court never receive it. So

Single-parent kids face different kinds of problems. For instance, they may have to take on more responsibilities, like making dinners or babysitting their brothers and sisters.

divorced women and their children have become what social scientists call the new poor.

As a result, s-p kids often have a great deal of responsibility. They have to do more household chores and often have to take care of younger siblings. They may not have time to do their schoolwork or time for themselves.

They may also suffer from a lack of attention, at least at first. Often, live-in parents are tired. They have to work and do all the jobs that used to be split between two parents. A single parent may not have the time or the energy for his or her kids.

Parents' dating makes some kids worry. They always hope their parents will get back together. When parents date, s-p kids fear their live-in parents are abandoning them as the absent parent did. They often try to get rid of the dates.

Sheila locked her mother's boyfriend out of the house. "The boyfriend laughed," she says. "Mom got mad. And it didn't get rid of the boyfriend. After a while, you realize that you aren't really being abandoned—which is what it feels like at first."

A parent marrying again can be a major problem, and a frequent one. Within three years of the end of the previous marriage, four out of five divorced or widowed men remarry. Three out of four women do.

Both of Danny's parents have remarried. He lives with his mother and stepfather. He spends vacations with his father and stepmother. "It's okay," he says.

Vivian's father remarried five years after her mother died. "It was nice to have another female in the house, but it wasn't easy to get used to," she says.

Brian's mother remarried. Every time he visits her, he's uncomfortable. Changes like this are difficult to get used to.

SOME SOLUTIONS

To resolve money problems, some single-parent families are living together. Other single parents exchange help or share the expense of paying for services. Two or three parents might share a baby-sitter, for instance. They help each other with big jobs. These arrangements cut living costs, and families don't feel so overwhelmed by all that needs doing.

Some s-p kids help with family money problems by learning how much such essentials as food and rent cost, and doing their share to stay within the budget. When they know how much money it takes to live, these children say they don't feel so frustrated when their parents say they can't afford something. Teenagers often try to get part-time jobs to pay for special clothes or entertainment.

Having too much responsibility can be a more difficult problem to solve. Sometimes only time helps. Little brothers and sisters get older. Then they don't have to be taken care of. They can begin to help with the chores. Even when siblings are small, their older brothers and sisters can teach them to pick up after themselves and to do simple chores.

Occasionally, a single parent will lean too heavily on a child. A mother may want her boy to become "the man of the house." A father may want his daughter to "be our little mother" now. A parent may confide in the children, telling them his or her problems. A parent may stop doing household jobs.

Becoming dependent on their children isn't something parents plan. It usually happens slowly, and nobody realizes it's happening. Social scientists say too many

Many single-parent kids say you have to keep an open mind.

kids live with the problem rather than talk to someone about it. They don't realize it isn't fair to themselves. The rules in single-parent families aren't always clear. It helps if they have s-p friends with whom to make comparisons. Sometimes, all they need to do is talk it over with their parents. If that doesn't work, a relative, counselor, teacher, or religious leader can help.

Giving up the idea of parents getting back together is also hard. Counselors say kids have to realize parents are entitled to their own lives.

"You have to keep an open mind," Jolene says. "Don't worry about things before they happen. Just because your parent dates someone doesn't mean they're going to get married. Sometimes you like the guy your mom is dating. Sometimes you think something is going to be terrible and then it isn't. It may not be easy, but it isn't as bad as you thought it would be."

When parents remarry, experts advise kids who are troubled by it to get counseling, however. Living with two adults again isn't the same as living with both parents. It's a new game. Everyone has new roles. Counselors can help make adjustment easier.

SCARY PROBLEMS AND WHO CAN HELP

Living in a single-parent family occasionally presents serious problems. But they all have solutions:

What if there isn't enough money to pay the rent or buy food and other necessities?

Families can contact government and church family services, which will provide money. They are listed in the telephone directory.

What happens if a parent has to go to the hospital and the kids are too young to stay by themselves?

If no other arrangements have been made, s-p kids may be placed in foster homes. Even though it is difficult to think of such things happening, it's important to make plans for emergencies. Sometimes the other parent or another relative can take care of the kids. S-p kids talk with their parents about whom to contact. They should also know how to contact them. Neighbors or friends might also be called on, or parents of a school friend.

Some problems can be even scarier than having a parent in the hospital. Occasionally, a child may have a parent who drinks too much. Or one who abuses the children.

When such things occur, s-p kids need to tell another adult—a counselor, coach, or teacher at school, a priest, pastor or rabbi, or somebody in the community. These things happen less often in single-parent families, but s-p kids are more vulnerable. There's not another adult around to see what is happening. Many kids mistakenly think it's their fault things have gone wrong. But s-p kids should never let themselves be treated badly.

"Reporting your parent for abusing you isn't easy," Julie explains. "Everybody asks a hundred questions. Sometimes you have to go to a foster home. You begin to wish you hadn't reported it, even though you know you had to. But you have to hang tough. It gets better."

Another frightening problem for s-p kids is not knowing what will happen to them if the parent they're living with should die. They already feel as though they've been abandoned once. They're afraid it can happen again. Counselors advise s-p kids to talk their fears over with their parents. It's hard to do, they agree, but it's necessary.

Having to face such serious possibilities is one reason single-parent kids become mature more quickly than their friends who live with both parents. They are also better able to take care of themselves.

Still another problem is kidnapping. Many parents who were not given custody of their children become angry. They snatch children away from the parents who have custody. Sometimes one parent may want to hurt the other parent, so he or she kidnaps the child. S-p kids need to know that kidnapping can happen and why a parent might do it.

Social scientists point out, though, that it's important for s-p kids to talk about their concerns and fears. If they can't talk to their parents, they should talk to another responsible adult. There *are* solutions to problems. They may not always be easy, but they're better than living with the problems. There's a lot of help available in most communities.

THE BRIGHT SIDE

Most s-p kids never wanted to be in single-parent families. But they also know it would be hard if they have to go back to living in two-parent families.

Once the tough, early days are over, s-p kids *like*

Parents and kids in single-parent families often do more things together than two-parent families do. They have more time for each other.

being more independent, more responsible, and more mature. They like knowing how to make decisions. They like knowing they can take care of themselves. They like having time to themselves. They like not having to listen to parents fight. They like being close to one parent. Some like having two houses to live in. "You don't get bored," Mac says.

In single-parent families, kids and parents often do more things together. When they lived with both parents, the likes and dislikes of two parents had to be considered. If one parent didn't like a certain activity, the family didn't do it.

For example, Nan's dad didn't like going to the movies. Now she and her mother go to the movies all the time. Jack's parents couldn't agree on where to go for their vacation, so they didn't go anywhere. Now he goes on trips with his dad. Helen's dad didn't like celebrations. Now her single-parent family has parties for even silly things—like the first snowfall.

Sometimes s-p kids fantasize about living in an ideal family. But they know that's only a dream. In real life, every family has its share of joys and problems.

"Be happy. It could be worse," Travis advises.

Once, being "different" was hard for many s-p kids. They felt alone. Now there are so many single-parent families, they're not alone anymore. As members of this new kind of family, they've discovered three things:

- The way a family is made doesn't make it good or not so good.
- You get more love and care when you give love and care.
- As long as you get love, security, and respect, you're living in a good family.

FOR MORE INFORMATION

For more information about single-parent families, write to:

International Youth Council
 of Parents Without Partners
7910 Woodmont Avenue
Bethesda, MD 20814

GLOSSARY/INDEX

ABSENT PARENT 9, 27, 31—*The parent with whom the child is not living.*

BROKEN HOME 32, 34—*A term formerly used to mean a family in which the parents are divorced.*

CHILD SUPPORT 10, 16, 36—*A term courts use to mean financial arrangements for caring for a child.*

CONCUBINE 14—*Women who live with men without being legally married to them.*

CUSTODY 9, 17, 18, 43—*The care and responsibility for the children after divorce.*

DESERTION 25—*Giving up, abandoning, or leaving without notice.*

HOUSEHOLD 7, 34—*Apartment or house in which someone lives.*

INTIMATE 12—*Being close to someone in love or friendship, having a close relationship with someone, to know someone or something very well.*

JOINT CUSTODY 9, 23—*A term courts use to mean that both parents, although divorced, are responsible for taking care of a child.*

LIVE-IN PARENT 9—*The parent with whom a child lives.*

ONE-PARENT KIDS 7—*Another term for single-parent kids.*

PATERNITY 12—*Fatherhood.*

GLOSSARY/INDEX

ROLE MODELS 35—*People who live good lives that one could pattern his or her life after.*

SINGLE-PARENT FAMILIES 5, 6, 8, 10, 15, 25, 32, 36, 38, 40, 41, 44—*Families headed by only one parent.*

SINGLE-PARENT HOUSEHOLD 7—*Apartment or house in which a child lives with one parent.*

SINGLE-PARENT KIDS 7, 8, 9, 16, 17, 19, 21, 22, 23, 24, 31, 32, 34, 35, 37, 38, 39, 40, 41, 42, 43, 45 — *Children who live in single-parent, or one-parent, families.*

SOCIAL SCIENTISTS 6, 7, 37, 39, 43—*People who study how people live and how their lives change and why.*

VISITATION RIGHTS 9—*A term used by courts for a parent's right to see his or her child.*